WE THE PEOPLE

The Lewis and Clark Expedition

by Patricia Ryon Quiri

Content Adviser: Professor Sherry L. Field,
Department of Social Science Education,
College of Education, The University of Georgia

Reading Adviser: Dr. Linda D. Labbo,
Department of Reading Education,
College of Education, The University of Georgia

COMPASS POINT BOOKS

Minneapolis, Minnesota

Compass Point Books
3722 West 50th Street, #115
Minneapolis, MN 55410

Visit Compass Point Books on the Internet at *www.compasspointbooks.com* or e-mail your request to *custserv@compasspointbooks.com*

Photographs ©: Corbis/Bettmann, cover; North Wind Picture Archives, 4; Archive Photos, 5; North Wind Picture Archives, 6; Independence National Historic Park, 8 top and bottom; Yale University/Beinecke Rare Book and Manuscript Library, 9; Smithsonian Institution/National Museum of American History, 10; Archive Photos, 14; North Wind Picture Archives/Nancy Carter, 15; North Wind Picture Archives, 16; North Wind Picture Archives/Nancy Carter, 17 top; North Wind Picture Archives, 17 bottom, 19, 20; North Wind Picture Archives/Nancy Carter, 21, 23; Wyoming Division of Cultural Resources, 24; North Wind Picture Archives, 25, 26; Tom Stack and Associates/John Shaw, 29; North Wind Picture Archives/Nancy Carter, 31; courtesy of Jefferson National Expansion Memorial/National Park Service, 32; FPG International, 34; Dave Schiefelbein, 37; Archive Photos, 38; Yale University/Beinecke Rare Book and Manuscript Library, 41.

Editors: E. Russell Primm and Emily J. Dolbear
Photo Researcher: Svetlana Zhurkina
Photo Selector: Dawn Friedman
Design: Bradfordesign, Inc.
Cartography: XNR Productions, Inc.

Library of Congress Cataloging-in-Publication Data

Quiri, Patricia Ryon.
    The Lewis and Clark Expedition / by Patricia Ryon Quiri.
        p. cm. — (We the people)
    Summary: Chronicles the expedition led by Lewis and Clark to explore the unknown western regions of America at the beginning of the nineteenth century, describing its mishaps, adventures, and impact on western expansion.
    ISBN 0-7565-0044-3
    1. Lewis and Clark Expedition (1804–1806)—Juvenile literature. 2. West (U.S.)—Discovery and exploration—Juvenile literature. [1. Lewis and Clark Expedition (1804–1806) 2. West (U.S.)—Discovery and exploration.] I. Title. II. We the people (Compass Point Books).
    F592.7 .Q57 2000
    917.804'2—dc21
                                                                                                00-008673

TABLE OF CONTENTS

A YOUNG COUNTRY

In 1803, the United States was just twenty-seven years old. Thomas Jefferson, author of the Declaration of Independence, was the third president of the young country. He was an intelligent president eager for the country to grow. Known as a "man of the people," Jefferson was well liked by most Americans.

On April 30, 1803, the United States, led by

Thomas Jefferson

4

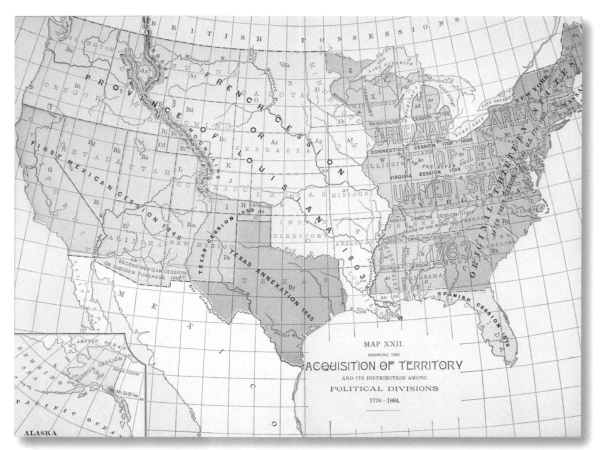

This map shows the boundaries of the Louisiana Purchase.

Thomas Jefferson, bought a large piece of land from France for about $15 million. The deal was called the Louisiana Purchase. It included land west of the Mississippi River to the Rocky Mountains.

The Rocky Mountains offered great chances to trap and trade fur.

The new land stretched from the Gulf of Mexico
to the Canadian border. The Louisiana Purchase
doubled the size of the United States.

PLANNING AN EXPEDITION

President Jefferson had big plans for the country's new land. He wanted to send an **expedition** to explore the area. He wanted to see if there was a water route between the Mississippi River and the Pacific Ocean. If such a water route existed, American traders could travel west to trade fur.

Jefferson also felt the land west of the Rocky Mountains, called Oregon Territory, would someday belong to the United States. Then the country would reach from the Atlantic Ocean all the way to the Pacific Ocean. With all that land, the young country would surely become a great and powerful nation.

Crossing thousands of miles of unmapped land and dealing with Native Americans would be a great challenge. Thomas Jefferson knew he needed intelligent, brave people to lead this expedition. The expedition would be called the Corps of Discovery.

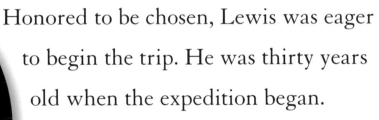

Meriwether Lewis

To head the Corps of Discovery, President Jefferson chose his personal secretary, former U.S. Army officer Meriwether Lewis. Lewis was a skilled outdoorsman. Honored to be chosen, Lewis was eager to begin the trip. He was thirty years old when the expedition began.

Lewis asked his best friend, William Clark, to join him. William Clark also had served in the U.S Army. He also had experience in the wilderness. He was thirty-four years old.

William Clark

PREPARING FOR THE EXPEDITION

In the winter of 1803, Lewis and Clark set up camp on the Mississippi River near St. Louis, Missouri. It was here that the group of about forty men began training and planning for the trip. The oldest was thirty-five, and the youngest was about seventeen. They built boats, got lots of exercise, and practiced

A list of supplies for the expedition

William Clark brought this compass on the expedition.

shooting. They packed supplies, including food, medicine, tools, and rifles.

The leaders of the group knew that many dangers lay ahead of them. They would have to deal with many Native American groups. If they could make friends with them, the Native Americans might share their knowledge of the land. So the men packed gifts such as beads, mirrors, pipes, knives, handkerchiefs, and belts.

Members of the expedition knew about hunting, steering down rivers, **blacksmithing**, making guns and bullets, and surviving in the wilderness. There was only one African-American man on the expedition. He was York, William Clark's slave.

10

THE START OF THE EXPEDITION

The Lewis and Clark expedition left St. Louis on May 14, 1804. The weather was fair and there was a gentle breeze.

They traveled in three boats. The largest was a 55-foot (17-meter)-long **keelboat** with one sail. A keelboat is a large wooden riverboat with a cabin built in the center. It needed twenty-two men to row. The other two boats were **pirogues**. These smaller boats were like canoes—one used seventy-one oars, the other only six.

The expedition also brought two horses, which were led along the riverbanks. The men planned to use them for hunting when food was in short supply.

11

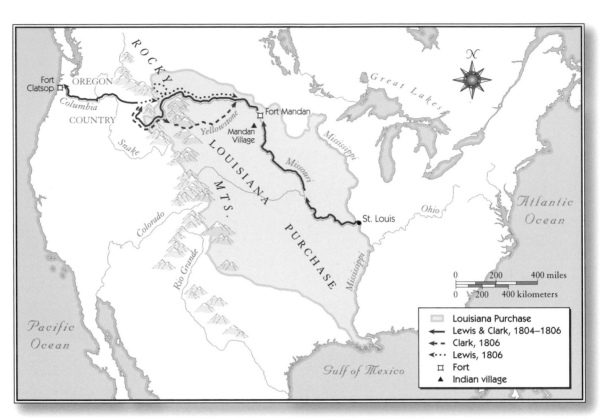

Map of the Lewis and Clark expedition

The original plan was to travel northwest along the Missouri River and reach the Rocky Mountains within about seven months—by the winter of 1804. From there, they would cross what they thought was a short **pass** to the

Columbia River, which would lead them to the Pacific Ocean by spring 1805. They planned to be back in St. Louis by the fall of 1805.

The trip was to take about a year and a half. However, it actually took Lewis and Clark more than two years and four months. They had no idea how huge the mountain ranges were.

Northwest travel along the Missouri River turned out to be more difficult than the leaders expected. The men had to deal with tree branches and rocks in the water. Mosquitoes and ticks plagued them. Only the smoke from campfires and smearing themselves with grease helped this problem.

Both Meriwether Lewis and William Clark were excellent leaders and outdoorsmen, but they

Meriwether Lewis was more serious than his friend, William Clark.

were very different in nature. Clark loved to talk and tell jokes. He usually supervised the boats.

Lewis was a very serious man and sometimes suffered from depression. Preferring to be alone, Lewis walked and explored the banks of the Missouri River with his dog, Seaman.

By August, the expedition had reached South Dakota. Buffalo were plentiful on the plains. They hunted and ate

14

Millions of buffalo such as these covered the Plains.

their first buffalo on August 23. They also enjoyed turkeys, geese, beaver, and fish.

Lewis and Clark kept detailed records for President Jefferson. They wrote down information

15

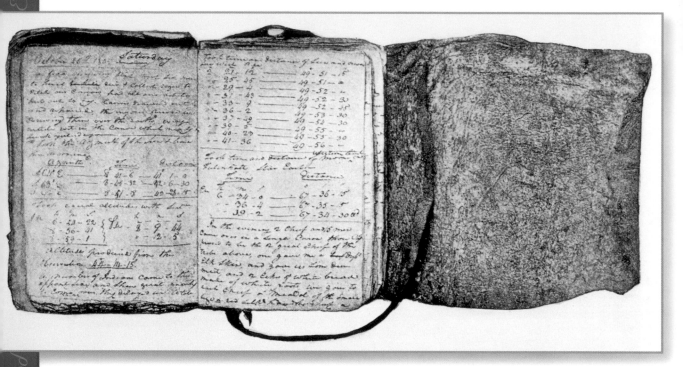

Clark recorded the expedition in this diary.

about the land, Native Americans, weather, animals, plants, and attitudes of the men. The animals of the plains included coyotes, prairie dogs, jackrabbits, and a kind of goat called a pronghorn—creatures that the men had never seen before.

Clark wrote about the pronghorn (right) and drew sketches of plants he saw.

apparently jointed Consisting) of 6 par and terminateing in one (in this form.) serrate, or like the teeth of a whip saw, each point terminateing in a small subulate spine, being from 25 to 27 in Numb.; veined, smoth, plain and of a deep green, their points tending obliquely towards the extremity of the rib or common footstalk. I do not know the fruit or flower of either. the 1st resembles a plant Common to many parts of the United States Called the Mountain Holly —.

Tuesday February 13th 1806.

The Clatsop left us this morning at 11. A.M. not

17

MEETING NATIVE AMERICANS

During August, the expedition met some Oto and Missouri people. Many of the Plains Indians lived in this large grassland region. The Oto and Missouri were friendly.

However, the men soon met the Sioux, who were not friendly. Even President Jefferson's message of peace offended them. The Sioux accepted the gifts, but the gifts caused problems too.

One Sioux chief felt that he didn't get enough and tried to take one of the expedition's boats. On shore were 100 of his men ready to fire bows and arrows. Lewis shouted to his men to aim their guns. Fortunately, the Sioux left.

By November, the explorers were in central North Dakota, home of the Mandan people. The

18

A Sioux camp

Mandan were pleased with their gifts. The two
groups made friends and smoked a peace pipe
together.

A Mandan village

Today's Fort Mandan

Because of the cold winter, the expedition decided to stay there until spring. They built a fort and called it Fort Mandan. Over the winter months, the men learned much about the Native American way of life and the land ahead.

21

A WOMAN NAMED SACAGAWEA

In April 1805, the Lewis and Clark expedition left Fort Mandan. The Mandan gave them a great send-off. They sang, danced, and exchanged gifts.

Toussaint Charbonneau, a French-Canadian fur trapper who lived among the Native Americans, joined the expedition. He would guide the expedition over the mountains and help the group communicate with the Native Americans.

Charbonneau was married to a young Shoshone girl named Sacagawea. She was about eighteen years old. The Shoshone lived near the Rocky Mountains and had many horses. When Sacagawea was about ten, the Minnitarree captured her and took her from her family.

A prairie footpath on Lewis and Clark's route

Sacagawea and her son, Pomp

Then Sacagawea was sold as a slave to Charbonneau, who made her one of his wives. Sacagawea and their two-month-old baby boy, nicknamed Pomp, joined the expedition too.

Perhaps Sacagawea would help the expedition get the horses they needed from the Shoshone. As it turned out, this young Shoshone girl contributed greatly to the Corps of Discovery.

The expedition now had two large pirogues and six small canoes. They sent the keelboat back down the river to St. Louis. The boat carried letters to President Jefferson about the journey

The expedition recorded seeing many plants, such as wild blue flax.

as well as samples of the animal and plant life discovered on the plains.

On May 14, 1805, exactly one year into their trip, a storm came up suddenly. One of the pirogues almost overturned when Charbonneau panicked. However, Sacagawea stayed calm and saved the items that had washed overboard. She was brave.

25

The expedition had to choose a fork in the river to reach the Great Falls in Montana.

A Fork in the River

On June 3, 1805, the group came to a fork in the river. Which of these was the Missouri? Which would lead to the Great Falls? Taking the wrong fork would mean losing valuable time. Lewis and Clark sent out teams to study each of the streams. They saw large green plains with herds of buffalo, elk, antelopes, and wolves. They could also see mountains, some of which were covered with snow.

Finally, after much thought, they chose one of the forks in the river. On about June 13, they reached the Great Falls in Montana. They had chosen the right stream. The region was familiar to Sacagawea, who had once lived on this land— the home of the Shoshone.

Obviously, they could not take the boats through the falls. They used cottonwood and willow trees to build trucks with wheels to carry the boats over land. It took about a month.

Soon after, Sacagawea became dangerously ill. Clark nursed her back to health. Lewis, too, became very ill. He boiled the twigs of a plant he described as the "choke cherry." Then he drank the strong black liquid. After only two doses, his fever went down and he was no longer in pain.

The group often came across wild animals. A brown bear once chased Lewis for 80 yards (73 m). Lewis finally ran into the river and the bear decided not to follow him.

Meriwether Lewis used the choke cherry plant to cure fever.

ANOTHER DECISION

In August 1805, the expedition came to another turning point in the Missouri. There the Missouri split into three different rivers. Again, a decision had to be made. Which river should they follow?

They chose the largest river and named it the Jefferson. The river **rapids** were so strong that at times they had to carry the canoes.

The group finally reached a stretch of high ground called the **Continental Divide**. At this point, the rivers flow west to the Pacific Ocean. On the other side of the Divide, the rivers flow east to the Mississippi.

Finally the party met Sacagawea's people—the Shoshone. She was overjoyed when the

Today's view of the Madison and Jefferson Rivers joining the Missouri

The expedition with Sacagawea's people, the Shoshone

chief turned out to be her long-lost brother, Cameahwait, whom she had believed to be dead. Having Sacagawea in the group told all Native Americans that the group came in peace. (Women were never part of a warring group.) Cameahwait sold the expedition the horses they needed to cross the dangerous Rocky Mountains.

As they began the crossing in late September 1805, the weather grew worse. Snow, freezing rain, and lack of animals to hunt made the journey even more difficult. Sacagawea's knowledge of roots to eat was helpful, but the men were starving. At times, they had to shoot their horses and mules for meat.

Meriwether Lewis sees the Rocky Mountains for the first time.

At last they completed their journey through the immense Rocky Mountains. They built five **dugout canoes,** as they had been taught by Native Americans, and entered the Snake River. They had to go through many rapids and over many cliffs. They lost precious supplies when some of the canoes overturned.

Things improved as the river grew wider and more gentle. Here they caught their fill of salmon, and animals were plentiful. The group ate well to regain their strength.

REACHING THE PACIFIC!

The expedition had now entered Oregon Territory. Although it was not part of the United States, Lewis and Clark's exploration of the area gave the United States claim to it.

The Snake River gave way to the Columbia River, which emptied into the Pacific Ocean. On November 7, 1805, the morning fog lifted, and the Lewis and Clark expedition could see the great sea and hear the thunderous waves breaking on the rocky shores. The men were filled with happiness and relief. They had reached their destination!

The group chose a place to build a camp for the winter. They called it Fort Clatsop, after the Native Americans who lived nearby.

The dramatic Oregon coast of the Pacific Ocean as it looks today

Fort Clatsop, where the Lewis and Clark expedition spent the winter of 1806

For more than four months, the men looked
for an American ship. They finally gave up hope
of returning by sea. They packed up and began
the return trip by land on March 23, 1806.

THE RETURN TRIP

On the way home, the expedition followed most of their previous route. But after the Rocky Mountains, Lewis and Clark split up to explore different routes. Clark went by the Three Forks into the Yellowstone River and Lewis took the unexplored Marias River to the north. They met at the Missouri River.

When the expedition reached the Mandan village in North Dakota, Sacagawea and Charbonneau decided to stay there. Much of the expedition's success had been because of Sacagewea. Her son, Pomp, was now more than one year old. Everyone had grown to love them and would miss them.

The expedition team finally returned to St. Louis on September 23, 1806. Huge crowds turned out to welcome them home as they sailed into the city. After nearly 2 ½ years, everyone had thought they were dead. Amazingly, they had lost only one member of their team. He had died of an illness three months into the journey.

The Lewis and Clark expedition had survived everything. They had lived through bad weather, starvation, illnesses, contact with more than fifty Native American groups, and many dangerous land and water crossings. Lewis had even been shot once in the rear end by one of his own men who mistook him for an elk!

They had traveled more than 7,689 miles (12,372 kilometers). Of course, it was a disappointment that a water route all the way to the Pacific

A field map of Lewis and Clark's route

Ocean did not exist. However, the journals kept by Lewis and Clark were priceless. They had made excellent maps as well as sketches of the land, rivers, plants, and animals.

Meriwether Lewis and William Clark led the greatest expedition in early American history. It paved the way for fur trappers, mountaineers, and settlers to go west. It gave the United States a claim to the land west of the Rocky Mountains. It paved the way for a stronger and wealthier United States that would stretch from the Atlantic Ocean all the way to the Pacific—"from sea to shining sea."

Glossary

blacksmithing—heating and hammering iron

Continental Divide—the stretch of high ground formed by the crests of the Rocky Mountains. Rivers on the east of it flow to the Atlantic and rivers on the west flow to the Pacific.

dugout canoes—canoes made by hollowing out large logs

expedition—a journey made for a specific purpose

keelboat—a large wooden riverboat with a cabin built in the center

pass—a low place in a mountain range

pirogues—boats like canoes

rapids—part of a river where the river flows very fast, usually over rocks

DID YOU KNOW?

- Meriwether Lewis spent $2,500 that he received from the U.S. Congress on almost two tons of goods for the expedition.

- The first and only person to die on the Lewis and Clark expedition, Sergeant Charles Floyd, was also the first U.S. soldier to die west of the Mississippi River.

- In their journals, Lewis and Clark described 178 plants and 122 animals that had never before been recorded for science.

- The buffalo were so plentiful in Montana, the group ate almost 9 pounds (4 kilograms) of buffalo meat a day.

IMPORTANT DATES

Timeline

1803	The United States doubles its size with the Louisiana Purchase on April 30.
1804	The expedition leaves St. Louis, Missouri, on May 14.
1805	The expedition leaves Fort Mandan in April; they choose a fork in the Missouri River in August; they reach the Pacific Ocean on November 7.
1806	The expedition begins the trip home on March 23; they return to St. Louis on September 23.

IMPORTANT PEOPLE

WILLIAM CLARK
(1770–1838), *American explorer*

THOMAS JEFFERSON
(1743–1826), *third U.S. president (1801–1809)*

MERIWETHER LEWIS
(1774–1809), *American explorer*

SACAGAWEA
(1787?–1812), *Shoshone guide and interpreter*

YORK
(?–1832?), *expedition member and slave of William Clark*

WANT TO KNOW MORE?

At the Library

Clark, William, and Peter and Connie Roop, eds. *Off the Map: The Journals of Lewis and Clark.* New York: Walker and Company, 1993.

Lourie, Peter. *In the Path of Lewis and Clark: Traveling the Missouri.* Parsippany, N.J.: Silver Burdett Press, 1997.

Morley, Jacqueline. *Across America—The Story of Lewis and Clark.* Danbury, Conn.: Franklin Watts, 1998.

Sanford, William R., and Carl R. Green. *Sacagawea: Native American Hero.* Springfield, N.J.: Enslow Publishers, 1997.

Streissguth, Thomas. *Lewis and Clark: Explorers of the Northwest.* Springfield, N.J.: Enslow Publishers, 1998.

On the Web

Lewis and Clark Journals Online

http://xroads.virginia.edu/~HYPER/JOURNALS/journals.html

To read the Lewis and Clark journals

Lewis and Clark Trail Heritage Foundation

http://www.lewisandclark.org/index.htm

For more about the expedition and for articles of interest

PBS Online: Lewis and Clark

http://www.pbs.org/lewisandclark/archive/time/index.html

For a timeline, pictures, and facts about the Lewis and Clark expedition

Through the Mail

Lewis & Clark National Historic Trail

1709 Jackson Street

Omaha, NE 68102-2571

For general information about visiting the expedition trail

On the Road

Lewis & Clark National Historic Trail Interpretive Center

4201 Giant Springs Road

Great Falls, MT 59403

406/727-8733

To see related exhibits, demonstrations of daily life on the expedition, and an introductory film by Ken Burns

INDEX

About the Author

A graduate of Alfred University in upstate New York, Patricia Ryon Quiri has a degree in elementary education and teaches second grade in the Pinellas County school system. She is the author of twenty-one children's books. Patricia Ryon Quiri lives with her husband, Bob, and their three sons in Oldsmar, Florida.